ESSAYS ON SUICIDE AND THE IMMORTALITY

David Hume

Table of Contents

ESSAYS ON SUICIDE AND THE IMMORTALITY

David Hume

Kessinger Publishing reprints thousands of hard–to–find books!

Visit us at http://www.kessinger.net

PREFACE

THESE two Essays on Suicide and the Immortality of the Soul, though not published in any edition of his works, are generally attributed to the late ingenious Mr. Hume.

The well–known contempt of this eminent philosopher for the common convictions of mankind, raised an apprehension of the contents from the very title of these pieces. But the celebrity of the author's name, renders them, notwithstanding, in some degree objects of great curiosity.

Owing to this circumstance, a few copies have been clandestinely circulated, at a large price, for some time, but without any comment. The very mystery attending this mode of selling them, made them more an object of request than they would otherwise have been. {iv}

The present publication comes abroad under no such restraint, and possesses very superior advantages. The annexed are intended to expose the sophistry contained in the original Essays, and may shew how little we have to fear from the adversaries of these great truths, from the pitiful figure which even Mr. Hume makes in thus violently exhausting his last strength in an abortive attempt to traduce or discredit them.

1

The two very matterly Letters from the Eloisa of Rosseau on the subject of , have been much celebrated, and we hope will be considered as materially increasing the value of this curious collection.

The admirers of will be pleased with seeing the remains of a favourite author rescued in this manner from that oblivion to which the prejudices of his countrymen had, in all appearance, consigned them; and even the religious part of mankind have some reason of triumph from the striking instance here given of truth's superiority to error, even when error has all the advantage of an elegant genius, and a great literary reputation to recommend it. {1}

ESSAY I. ON SUICIDE.

ONE considerable advantage that arises from Philosophy, consists in the sovereign antidote which it affords to superstition and false religion. All other remedies against that pestilent distemper are vain, or at least uncertain. Plain good sense and the practice of the world, which alone serve most purposes of life, are here found ineffectual: History as well as daily experience furnish instances of men endowed with the {2} strongest capacity for business and affairs, who have all their lives crouched under slavery to the grossest superstition. Even gaiety and sweetness of temper, which infuse a balm into every other wound, afford no remedy to so virulent a poison; as we may particularly observe of the fair sex, who tho' commonly possest of their rich presents of nature, feel many of their joys blasted by this importunate intruder. But when found Philosophy has once gained possession of the mind, superstition is effectually excluded, and one may fairly affirm that her triumph over this enemy is more complete than over most of the vices and imperfections incident to human nature. Love or anger, ambition or avarice, have their root in the temper and affection, which the soundest reason is scarce ever able fully to correct, but superstition being founded on false opinion, must immediately vanish when true philosophy has inspired juster sentiments of superior powers. The contest is here more equal between the distemper and the medicine, {3} and nothing can hinder the latter from proving effectual but its being false and sophisticated.

IT will here be superfluous to magnify the merits of Philosophy by displaying the pernicious tendency of that vice of which it cures the human mind. The superstitious man says Tully[1] is miserable in every scene, in every incident in life; even sleep itself, which banishes all other cares of unhappy mortals, affords to him matter of new terror; while he examines his dreams, and finds in those visions of the night prognostications of future calamities. I may add that tho' death alone can put a full period to his misery, he dares not fly to this refuge, but still prolongs a miserable existence from a vain fear left he offend his Maker, by using the power, with which that beneficent being has endowed him. The presents of God and nature are ravished from us by this {4} cruel enemy, and notwithstanding that one step would remove us from the regions of pain and sorrow, her menaces still chain us down to a hated being which she herself chiefly contributes to render miserable.

'TIS observed by such as have been reduced by the calamities of life to the necessity of employing this fatal remedy, that if the unseasonable care of their friends deprive them of that species of Death which they proposed to themselves, they seldom venture upon any other, or can summon up so much resolution a second time as to execute their purpose. So great is our horror of death, that when it presents itself under any form, besides that to which a man has endeavoured to reconcile his imagination, it acquires new terrors and overcomes his feeble courage: But when the menaces of superstition are joined to this natural timidity, no wonder it quite deprives men of all power over their lives, since even many pleasures and enjoyments, {5} to which we are carried by a strong propensity, are torn from us by this inhuman tyrant. Let us here endeavour to restore men to their native liberty, by examining all the common arguments against Suicide, and shewing that that action may be free from every imputation of guilt or blame, according to the sentiments of all the antient philosophers.

IF Suicide be criminal, it must be a transgression of our duty either to God, our neighbour, or ourselves. — To prove that suicide is no transgression of our duty to God, the following considerations may perhaps suffice. In order to govern the material world, the almighty Creator has established general and immutable laws, by which all bodies, from the greatest planet to the smallest particle of matter, are maintained in their proper sphere and function. To govern the animal world, he has endowed all living creatures with bodily and mental powers; with senses, passions, {6} appetites, memory, and judgement, by which they are impelled or regulated in that course of life to which they are destined. These two distinct principles of the material and animal world, continually encroach upon each other, and mutually retard or forward each others operation. The powers of men and of all other animals are restrained and directed by the nature and qualities of the surrounding bodies, and the modifications and actions of these bodies are incessantly altered by the operation of all animals. Man is stopt by rivers in his passage over the surface of the earth; and rivers, when properly directed, lend their force to the motion of machines, which serve to the use of man. But tho' the provinces of the material and animal powers are not kept entirely separate, there results from thence no discord or disorder in the creation; on the contrary, from the mixture, union, and contrast of all the various powers of inanimate bodies and living creatures, arises that sympathy, harmony, {7} and proportion, which affords the surest argument of supreme wisdom. The providence of the Deity appears not immediately in any operation, but governs every thing by those general and immutable laws, which have been established from the beginning of time. All events, in one sense, may be pronounced the action of the Almighty, they all proceed from those powers with which he has endowed his creatures. A house which falls by its own weight, is not brought to ruin by his providence, more than one destroyed by the hands of men; nor are the human faculties less his workmanship, than the laws of motion and gravitation. When the passions play, when the judgment dictates, when the limbs obey; this is all the operation of God, and upon these animate principles, as well as upon the inanimate, has he established the government of the universe. Every event is alike important in the eyes of that infinite being, who takes in at one glance the most distant regions of space, and {8} remotest periods of time. There is no event, however important to us, which he has exempted from the general laws that govern the universe, or which he has peculiarly reserved for his own immediate action and operation. The revolution of states and empires depends upon the smallest caprice or passion of single men; and the lives of men are shortened or extended by the smallest accident of air or dies, sunshine or tempest. Nature still continues her progress and operation; and if general laws be ever broke by particular volitions of the Deity, 'tis after a manner which entirely escapes human observation. As on the one hand, the elements and other inanimate parts of the creation carry on their action without regard to the particular interest and situation of men; so men are entrusted to their own judgment and discretion in the various shocks of matter, and may employ every faculty with which they are endowed, in order to provide for their ease, happiness, or {9} preservation. What is the meaning then of that principle, that a man who tired of life, and hunted by pain and misery, bravely overcomes all the natural terrors of death, and makes his escape from this cruel scene: that such a man I say, has incurred the indignation of his Creator by encroaching on the office of divine providence, and disturbing the order of the universe? Shall we assert that the Almighty has reserved to himself in any peculiar manner the disposal of the lives of men, and has not submitted that event, in common with others, to the general laws by which the universe is governed? This is plainly false; the lives of men depend upon the same laws as the lives of all other animals; and these are subjected to the general laws of matter and motion. The fall of a tower, or the infusion of a poison, will destroy a man equally with the meanest creature; an inundation sweeps away every thing without distinction that comes within the reach of its fury. Since therefore the lives of men {10} are for ever dependant on the general laws of matter and motion, is a man's disposing of his life criminal, because in every case it is criminal to encroach upon these laws, or disturb their operation? But this seems absurd; all animals are entrusted to their own prudence and skill for their conduct in the world, and have full authority as far as their power extends, to alter all the operations of nature. Without the excercise of this authority they could not subsist a moment; every action, every motion of a man, innovates on the order of some parts of matter, and diverts from their ordinary course the general laws of motion. Putting together, therefore, these conclusion, we find that human life depends upon the general laws of matter and motion, and that it is no encroachment on the office of providence to disturb or alter these general laws: Has not every one, of consequence, the free disposal of his own life? And may he not lawfully employ that power with which nature has endowed him? In order {11} to destroy the evidence of this conclusion, we must shew a reason why this particular cafe is excepted; is it because human life is of such great importance, that 'tis a presumption for human prudence to dispose of it? But the life of a man is of no greater importance to the universe than that of an oyster. And were it of ever so great importance, the order of human nature has actually submitted it to human prudence, and reduced us to a necessity, in every incident, of determining concerning it. — Were the disposal of human life so much reserved as the peculiar province of the Almighty, that it were an encroachment on his right, for men to dispose of their own lives; it would be equally criminal to act for the preservation of life as for its destruction. If I turn aside a stone which is falling upon my head, I disturb the course of nature, and I invade the peculiar province of the Almighty, by lengthening out my life beyond the period which by the general laws of matter and motion he had assigned it. {12}

A hair, a fly, an insect is able to destroy this mighty being whose life is of such importance. Is it an absurdity to suppose that human prudence may lawfully dispose of what depends on such insignificant causes? It would be no crime in me to divert the or from its course, were I able to effect such purposes. Where then is the crime of turning a few ounces of blood from their natural channel? — Do you imagine that I repine at Providence or curse my creation, because I go out of life, and put a period to a being, which, were it to continue, would render me miserable? Far be such sentiments from me;

I am only convinced of a matter of fact, which you yourself acknowledge possible, that human life may be unhappy, and that my existence, if further prolonged, would become ineligible; but I thank Providence, both for the good which I have already enjoyed, and for the power with which I am endowed of escaping the ill that {13} threatens me.[2] To you it belongs to repine at providence, who foolishly imagine that you have no such power, and who must still prolong a hated life, tho' loaded with pain and sickness, with shame and poverty — Do not you teach, that when any ill befals me, tho' by the malice of my enemies, I ought to be resigned to providence, and that the actions of men are the operations of the Almighty as much as the actions of inanimate beings? When I fall upon my own sword, therefore, I receive my death equally from the hands of the Deity as if it had proceeded from a lion, a precipice, or a fever. The submission which you require to providence, in every calamity that befals me, excludes not human skill and industry, if possible by their means I can avoid or escape the calamity: And why may I not employ one remedy as well as another? — If my life be not my own, it were criminal for me to put it in danger, as {14} well as to dispose of it; nor could one man deserve the appellation of , whom glory or friendship transports into the greatest dangers, and another merit the reproach of or who puts a period to his life, from the same or like motives. — There is no being, which possesses any power or faculty, that it receives not from its Creator, nor is there any one, which by ever so irregular an action can encroach upon the plan of his providence, or disorder the universe. Its operations are his works equally with that chain of events which it invades, and which ever principle prevails, we may for that very reason conclude it to be most favoured by him. Be it animate, or inanimate, rational, or irrational, 'tis all a cafe: its power is still derived from the supreme Creator, and is alike comprehended in the order of his providence. When the horror of pain prevails over the love of life; when a voluntary action anticipates the effects of blind causes, 'tis only in consequence of those {15} powers and principles which he has implanted in his creatures. Divine providence is still inviolate, and placed far beyond the reach of human injuries. 'Tis impious says the old Roman superstition[3] to divert rivers from their course, or invade the prerogatives of nature. 'Tis impious says the French superstition to inoculate for the small–pox, or usurp the business of providence by voluntarily producing distempers and maladies. 'Tis impious says the modern superstition, to put a period to our own life, and thereby rebel against our Creator; and why not impious, say I, to build houses, cultivate the ground, or fail upon the ocean? In all these actions we employ our powers of mind and body, to produce some innovation in the course of nature; and in none of them do we any more. They are all of them therefore equally innocent, or equally criminal. . — I ask, why do you conclude that providence has placed me in this station?

For my part I find that I owe my birth to a long chain of causes, of which many depended upon voluntary actions of men. . If so, then neither does my death, however voluntary, happen without its consent; and whenever pain or sorrow so far overcome my patience, as to make me tired of life, I may conclude that I am recalled from my station in the clearest and most express terms. 'Tis providence surely that has placed me at this present in this chamber: But may I not leave it when I think proper, without being liable to the imputation of having deserted my post or station? When I shall be dead, the principles of {17} which I am composed will still perform their part in the universe, and will be equally useful in the grand fabrick, as when they composed this individual creature. The difference to the whole will be no greater than betwixt my being in a chamber and in the open air. The one change is of more importance to me than the other; but not more so to the universe.

— 'TIS a kind of blasphemy to imagine that any created being can disturb the order of the world, or invade the business of Providence! It supposes, that that being possesses powers and faculties, which it received not from its creator, and which are not subordinate to his government and authority. A man may disturb society no doubt, and thereby incur the displeasure of the Almighty: But the government of the world is placed far beyond his reach and violence. And how does it appear that the Almighty is displeased with those actions that disturb society? By the principles {18} which he has implanted in human nature, and which inspire us with a sentiment of remorse if we ourselves have been guilty of such actions, and with that of blame and disapprobation, if we ever observe them in others: — Let us now examine, according to the method proposed, whether Suicide be of this kind of actions, and be a breach of our duty to our and to .

A MAN who retires from life does no harm to society: He only ceases to do good; which, if it is an injury, is of the lowest kind. — All our obligations to do good to society seem to imply something reciprocal. I receive the benefits of society, and therefore ought to promote its interests; but when I withdraw myself altogether from society, can I be bound any longer? But allowing that our obligations to do good were perpetual, they have certainly some bounds; I am not obliged to do a small good to society at the expence of a {19} great harm to myself; why then should I prolong a miserable existence, because of some frivolous advantage which the public may perhaps receive from me? If upon account of age and infirmities, I may lawfully resign any office, and employ my time altogether in fencing against these calamities, and alleviating, as much as possible, the miseries of my future life: why may I not cut short these miseries at once by an action which is no more prejudicial to society? — But suppose that it is no longer in my power to promote the interest of society, suppose that I am a burden to it, suppose that my life hinders some person from being much more useful to society. In such cases, my resignation of life must not only be innocent, but laudable. And most people who lie under any temptation to abandon existence, are in some such situation; those who have health, or power, or authority, have commonly better reason to be in humour with the world. {20}

A MAN is engaged in a conspiracy for the public interest; is seized upon suspicion; is threatened with the rack; and knows from his own weakness that the secret will be extorted from him: Could such a one consult the public interest better than by putting a quick period to a miserable life? This was the case of the famous and brave of . — Again, suppose a malefactor is justly condemned to a shameful death, can any reason be imagined, why he may not anticipate his punishment, and save himself all the anguish of thinking on its dreadful approaches? He invades the business of providence no more than the magistrate did, who ordered his execution; and his voluntary death is equally advantageous to society, by ridding it of a pernicious member.

THAT Suicide may often be consistent with interest and with our duty to ourselves, no one can question, who allows that age, {21} sickness, or misfortune, may render life a burthen, and make it worse even than annihilation. I believe that no man ever threw away life, while it was worth keeping. For such is our natural horror of death, that small motives will never be able to reconcile us to it; and though perhaps the situation of a man's health or fortune did not seem to require this remedy, we may at least be assured that any one who, without apparent reason, has had recourse to it, was curst with such an incurable depravity or gloominess of temper as must poison all enjoyment, and render him equally miserable as if he had been loaded with the most grievous misfortunes. — If suicide be supposed a crime, 'tis only cowardice can impel us to it. If it be no crime, both prudence and courage should engage us to rid ourselves at once of existence, when it becomes a burthen. 'Tis the only way that we can then be useful to society, by setting an example, which if imitated, would preserve to every one his chance for happiness in life, {22} and would effectually free him from all danger of misery.[4]{23}

ESSAY II. ON THE IMMORTALITY OF THE SOUL.

BY the mere light of reason it seems difficult to prove the of the ; the arguments for it are commonly derived either from topics, or or . But in reality 'tis the Gospel and the Gospel alone, that has brought .

I. METAPHYSICAL topics suppose that the soul is immaterial, and that 'tis impossible {24} for thought to belong to a material substance. — But just metaphysics teach us that the notion of substance is wholly confused and imperfect, and that we have no other idea of any substance, than as an aggregate of particular qualities, inhering in an unknown something. Matter, therefore, and spirit, are at bottom equally unknown, and we cannot determine what qualities inhere in the one or in the other. They likewise teach us that nothing can be decided concerning any cause or effect, and that experience being the only source of our judgements of this nature, we cannot know from any other principle, whether matter, by its structure or arrangement, may not be the cause of thought. Abstract reasonings cannot decide any question of fact or existence. — But admitting a spiritual substance to be dispersed throughout the universe, like the etherial fire of the , and to be the only inherent subject of thought, we have reason to conclude {25} from that nature uses it after the manner she does the other substance, . She employs it as a kind of paste or clay; modifies it into a variety of forms and existences; dissolves after a time each modification, and from its substance erects a new form. As the same material substance may successively compose the bodies of all animals, the same spiritual substance may compose their minds: Their consciousness, or that system of thought which they formed during life, may be continually dissolved by death. And nothing interests them in the new modification. The most positive asserters of the mortality of the soul, never denied the immortality of its substance. And that an immaterial substance, as well as a material, may lose its memory or consciousness, appears in part from experience, if the soul be immaterial. — Reasoning from the common course of nature, and without supposing any new interposition of the supreme cause, which ought always to be excluded from philosophy, {26} what is incorruptible must also be ingenerable. The Soul therefore if immortal, existed before our birth; and if the former existence no ways concerned us, neither will the latter. — Animals undoubtedly feel, think, love, hate, will, and even reason, tho' in a more imperfect manner than men; are their souls also immaterial and immortal?

9

II. LET us now consider the moral arguments, chiefly those derived from the justice of God, which is supposed to be farther interested in the farther punishment of the vicious and reward of the virtuous. — But these arguments are grounded on the supposition that God has attributes beyond what he has exerted in this universe, with which alone we are acquainted. Whence do we infer the existence of these attributes? — 'Tis very safe for us to affirm, that whatever we know the Deity to have actually done, is best; but 'tis very dangerous to affirm, that he must always do {27} what to us seems best. In how many instances would this reasoning fail us with regard to the present world? — But if any purpose of nature be clear, we may affirm, that the whole scope and intention of man's creation, so far as we can judge by natural reason, is limited to the present life. With how weak a concern from the original inherent structure of the mind and passions, does he ever look farther? What comparison either for steadiness or efficacy, betwixt so floating an idea, and the most doubtful persuasion of any matter of fact that occurs in common life. There arise indeed in some minds some unaccountable terrors with regard to futurity; but these would quickly vanish were they not artificially fostered by precept and education. And those who foster them, what is their motive? Only to gain a livelihood, and to acquire power and riches in this world. Their very zeal and industry therefore is an argument against them. {28}

WHAT cruelty, what iniquity, what injustice in nature, to confine all our concern, as well as all our knowledge, to the present life, if there be another scene still waiting us, of infinitely greater consequence? Ought this barbarous deceit to be ascribed to a beneficent and wife being? — Observe with what exact proportion the task to be performed and the performing powers are adjusted throughout all nature. If the reason of man gives him great superiority above other animals, his necessities are proportionably multiplied upon him; his whole time, his whole capacity, activity, courage, and passion, find sufficient employment in fencing against the miseries of his present condition, and frequently, nay almost always are too slender for the business assigned them. — A pair of shoes perhaps was never yet wrought to the highest degree of perfection which that commodity is capable of attaining. Yet it is necessary, at least very useful, that there should be some politicians and moralists, {29} even some geometers, poets, and philosophers among mankind. The powers of men are no more superior to their wants, considered merely in this life, than those of foxes and hares are, compared to wants and to their period of existence. The inference from parity of reason is therefore obvious. —

ON the theory of the Soul's mortality, the inferiority of women's capacity is easily accounted for. Their domestic life requires no higher faculties, either of mind or body. This circumstance vanishes and becomes absolutely insignificant, on the religious theory: the one sex has an equal task to perform as the other; their powers of reason and resolution ought also to have been equal, and both of them infinitely greater than at present. As every effect implies a cause, and that another, till we reach the first cause of all, which is the Deity; every thing that happens is ordained by him, and nothing can be the object of his punishment or vengeance. — By what rule are punishments {30} and rewards distributed? What is the divine standard of merit and demerit? shall we suppose that human sentiments have place in the Deity? How bold that hypothesis. We have no conception of any other sentiments. — According to human sentiments, sense, courage, good manners, industry, prudence, genius, are essential parts of personal merits. Shall we therefore erect an elysium for poets and heroes like that of the antient mythology? Why confine all rewards to one species of virtue? Punishment, without any proper end or purpose, is inconsistent with ideas of goodness and justice, and no end can be served by it after the whole scene is closed. Punishment, according to conception, should bear some proportion to the offence. Why then eternal punishment for the temporary offences of so frail a creature as man? Can any one approve of 's rage, who intended to extirminate a whole nation because they had seized his favorite horse Bucephalus?[5] {31}

HEAVEN and Hell suppose two distinct species of men, the good and the bad; but the greatest part of mankind float betwixt vice and virtue. — Were one to go round the world with an intention of giving a good supper to the righteous, and a sound drubbing to the wicked, he would frequently be embarrassed in his choice, and would find that the merits and the demerits of most men and women scarcely amount to the value of either. — To suppose measures of approbation and blame different from the human confounds every thing. Whence do we learn that there is such a thing as moral distinctions, but from our own sentiments? — What man who has not met with personal provocation (or what good–natured man who has) could inflict on crimes, from the sense of blame alone, even the common, legal, frivolous punishments? And does any thing steel the breast of judges and juries against the sentiments of humanity but reflection on necessity and public interest? {32} By the Roman law those who had been guilty of parricide and confessed their crime, were put into a sack alone with an ape, a dog, and a serpent, and thrown into the river. Death alone was the punishment of those whose who denied their guilt, however fully proved. A criminal was tried before , and condemned after a full conviction, but the humane emperor, when he put the last interrogatory, gave it such a turn as to lead the wretch into a denial of his guilt. "You surely (said the "prince) did not kill your father."[6] This lenity suits our natural ideas of even towards the greatest of all criminals, and even though it prevents so inconsiderable a sufference. Nay even the most bigotted priest would naturally without reflection approve of it, provided the crime was not heresy or infidelity; for as these crimes hurt himself in his interest and advantages, perhaps he may not be altogether so {33} indulgent to them. The chief source of moral ideas is the reflection on the interest of human society. Ought these interests, so short, so frivolous, to be guarded by punishments eternal and infinite? The damnation of one man is an infinitely greater evil in the universe, than the subversion of a thousand millions of kingdoms. Nature has rendered human infancy peculiarly frail and mortal, as it were on purpose to refute the notion of a probationary state; the half of mankind die before they are rational creatures.

III. THE arguments from the analogy of nature are strong for the mortality of the soul, and are really the only philosophical arguments which ought to be admitted with regard to this question, or indeed any question of fact. — Where any two objects are so closely connected that all alterations which we have ever seen in the one, are attended with proportionable alterations in the other; we ought to conclude {34} by all rules of analogy, that, when there are still greater alterations produced in the former, and it is totally dissolved, there follows a total dissolution of the latter. — Sleep, a very small effect on the body, is attended with a temporary extinction, at least a great confusion in the soul. — The weakness of the body and that of the mind in infancy are exactly proportioned, their vigour in manhood, their sympathetic disorder in sickness; their common gradual decay in old age. The step further seems unavoidable; their common dissolution in death. The last symptoms which the mind discovers are disorder, weakness, insensibility, and stupidity, the fore–runners of its annihilation. The farther progress of the same causes encreasing, the same effects totally extinguish it. Judging by the usual analogy of nature, no form can continue when transferred to a condition of life very different from the original one, in which it was placed. Trees perish in the water, fishes in the air, animals in the earth. Even so small a difference as that of climate is often {35} fatal. What reason then to imagine, that an immense alteration, such as is made on the soul by the dissolution of its body and all its organs of thought and sensation, can be effected without the dissolution of the whole? Every thing is in common betwixt soul and body. The organs of the one are all of them the organs of the other. The existence therefore of the one must be dependant on that of the other. — The souls of animals are allowed to be mortal; and these bear so near a resemblance to the souls of men, that the analogy from one to the other forms a very strong argument. Their bodies are not more resembling; yet no one rejects the argument drawn from comparative anatomy. The is therefore the only system of this kind that philosophy can harken to.

NOTHING in this world is perpetual, every thing however seemingly firm is in continual flux and change, the world itself gives symptoms of frailty and dissolution. How contrary to analogy, therefore, to imagine {36} that one single from, seemingly the frailest of any, and subject to the greatest disorders, is immortal and indissoluble? What daring theory is that! how lightly, not to say how rashly entertained! How to dispose of the infinite number of posthumous existences ought also to embarrass the religious theory. Every planet in every solar system we are at liberty to imagine peopled with intelligent mortal beings, at least we can fix on no other supposition. For these then a new universe must every generation be created beyond the bounds of the present universe, or one must have been created at first so prodigiously wise as to admit of this continual influx of beings. Ought such bold suppositions to be received by any philosophy, and that merely on there pretext of a bare possibility? When it is asked whether , , and every stupid clown that ever existed in , , or , are now alive; can any man think, that a scrutiny of nature will furnish arguments {37} strong enough to answer so strange a question in the affirmative? The want of argument without revelation sufficiently establishes the negative. — " (says [7]) "." Our insensibility before the composition of the body, seems to natural reason a proof of a like state after dissolution. Were our horrors of annihilation an original passion, not the effect of our general love of happiness, it would rather prove the mortality of the soul. For as nature does nothing in vain, she would never give us a horror against an impossible event. She may give us a horror against an unavoidable; yet the human species could not be preserved had not nature inspired us with and aversion toward it. All doctrines are to be suspected which are favoured by {38} our passions, and the hopes and fears which gave rise to this doctrine are very obvious.

'TIS an infinite advantage in every controversy to defend the negative. If the question be out of the common experienced course of nature, this circumstance is almost if not altogether decisive. By what arguments or analogies can we prove any state of existence, which no one ever saw, and which no way resembles any that ever was seen? Who will repose such trust in any pretended philosophy as to admit upon its testimony the reality of so marvellous a scene? Some new species of logic is requisite for that purpose, and some new faculties of the mind, that may enable us to comprehend that logic.

ESSAYS ON SUICIDE AND THE IMMORTALITY

NOTHING could set in a fuller light the infinite obligations which mankind have to divine revelation, since we find that no other medium could ascertain this great and important truth. {39}

ANTI SUICIDE.

(1) THIS elaborate eulogium on philosophy points obliquely at religion, which we christians consider as the only sovereign antidote to every disease incident to the mind of man. It is indeed hard to say what reason might do were it freed from all restraints, especially if a succession of philosophers were incessantly improving on one another as they went on, avoiding and correcting the mistakes of those who preceded them in the same pursuit, till at last one complete and rational system was effected. Great things might probably be accomplished in this manner. But no such plan in fact ever was or is likely to be finished. Neither priestcraft, nor magisterial powers, however, cramped the progress of improving reason, or baffled the genius of enquiring man. The principles of religion and virtue were freely canvassed by the boldest spirits of antiquity. In truth, the superior advantage and necessity of the christian religion seems manifest from this particular circumstance, {40} that it has taken away every possible restraint from natural religion, allowing it to exert itself to the utmost in finding out the fundamental truths of virtue, and in acquiescing in them, in openly avowing and acknowledging them when revealed, in extending the views and expectations of men, in giving them more just and liberal sentiments, and in publickly and uniformly disclaiming any intention of establishing a kingdom for its votaries or believers in this world.

THE doctrines of the gospel are not intended to instruct us in the knowledge of every thing which may be really useful in the present life, far less of every thing, which, from curiosity alone, we may have a mighty desire to know. Revelation considers mankind in their highest capacity, as the rational and accountable subjects of God, and as capable both of present and future happiness or misery, according to their behaviour. Its chief, if not its sole design, is to give us those views and impressions of our nature, of our state, of the perfections, the counsels, the laws, and the government of God, which, under the influence of providence, are the immediate and infallible means of the purity, of the comfort, and of the moral order, rectitude, and excellence of our immortal souls. As corrupted and disordered, we are incapable of true happiness, till purified and restored to order. As guilty and {41} mortal creatures, we can have no true consolation without the hopes of pardon in a future and seperate state of existence. As surrounded with dangers, and obnoxious to every dismal apprehension, we can possess no solid, or permanent content, but in the sincere and well grounded convictions of that gracious and righteous administration so minutely and explicitly delineated in the scriptures. It is evident, therefore, that the principal excellence and utility of revealed truths upon the sanctification and consolation of our hearts. They tally exactly with the present circumstances of mankind, and are admirably adapted to cure every disease, every disorder of the human mind, to beget, to cherish, and confirm every pure, every virtuous, every pious disposition.

MANKIND are certainly at present in a state of the deepest corruption and depravity, and at the same time apt to continue strangely insensible of the misery and danger to which, under the government of infinite wisdom, it necessarily renders them. Nothing can be conceived more fit to rouse them from their lethargy, and to awaken them to a just sense of their condition, than a messenger from Heaven, clothed with divine authority, setting before them the intrinsic {42} baseness, malignity, and wretchedness of vice, together with the certain, the dreadful, the eternal consequences of continuing in it.

COULD we enter upon a particular view of all those maladies and disorders which infest and destroy the souls of men, it were easy to shew, that a steadfast belief of religion is, in truth, the most natural and the best antidote or remedy for each of them. It is obvious, or least, that the clear and full manifestation, which the gospel has given of the character of God, and the laws of his moral government, and of the terms of salvation through faith in the religion of his son, are all finely calculated to root out the principles of superstition, and all false notions, destructive to the virtue and happiness of mankind, and to plant in their room whatever has a natural and direct tendency to promote our virtue, our perfection, our felicity.

(2) CLEOMENES, king of Sparta, when suffering under misfortune, was advised to kill himself by Tharyceon. "Thinkest thou, wicked man, (said he) to shew thy fortitude by rushing upon death, an expedient always at hand, the dastardly resource of the {43} basest minds? Better than we, by the fortune of arms, or overpowered by numbers, have left the field of battle to their enemies; but he who, to avoid pain, or calamity, or censures of men, gives up the contest, we are to seek death, that death ought to be in action. It is base to live or die only for ourselves. All we gain by suicide is to get our own reputation, or doing the least service to our country. In hopes, then, we may yet be of some use to others, both methinks are bound to preserve life as long as we can. Whenever these hopes

shall have altogether abandoned us, death, if sought for, will readily be found.

(3) OF all the refines cobwebs, to which sophistry has given birth, this seems at once the most elaborate and the most flimsy. It seems one of the first and most indisputable maxims in all found reasoning, that no ideas whatever should have a place in the premises, which do not communicate a sensible energy to the conclusion. But where is the connection between the beginning and end of this wire–drawn argument. What have the various beautiful facts, thus elegantly stated, to do with a man's taking away his own {44} life? Though the greatest philosopher be of no more consequence to the general system of things than an oyster, and though the life of the one were, in every respect, as perfectly insignificant as that of the other, still the meanest of mankind is not without importance in his own eyes. And where is he who is guided uniformly, in all his actions, more by a sense of his relation to the universe at large, than by the value he retains for himself, or the deference he has to his own opinion.

NO deduction, however plausible, can produce conviction in any rational mind, which originates in a supposition grossly absurd. Is it possible to conceive the author of nature capable of authenticating a deed, which ultimately terminates in the total annihilation of the system? By which of the creatures beneath us is the first law of their being thus daringly violated? And if suicide be eligible to man, under any possible misfortune or distress, why not to them? Are not they also subject to the various miseries which arise from wayward accidents and hostile elements? Why, therefore, open a door for our escape from those evils of which others have their share, to whom, however, it must remain for ever shut? {45}

IN truth, the existence of all animals depends entirely on their inviolable attachment to self–preservation. Their attention to all is accordingly the obvious and common condition of all their natures. By this great and operative principle nature has chiefly consulted her own safety. Our philosopher's notions are so extremely hostile to her most essential institutions, that she could not possibly survive a general conviction of them. And, in spite of all the sophistry he is master of, the question here will eternally recur, whether the wisdom of nature, or the philosophy of our author, deserves the preference.

(4) THIS apology for the commission, arising from man's insignificance in the moral world, from the reciprocation of social duty being dissolved, or from the benefit resulting from the voluntary dismission of being, is contrary to the soundest principles of

16

jurisprudence, to the condition of human nature, and to the general establishment of things.

THAT a man who retires from life , does no harm to society, is a proposition peculiarly absurd and erroneous. What is {46} lawful for one, may be lawful for all, and no society can subsist in the conviction of a principle thus hostile to its being.

IT seems to be a maxim in human existence, that no creature has a right to decide peremptorily on the importance, utility, or necessity of his own being. There are an infinite variety of secret connections and associations in the vast system of things, which the eye of created wisdom cannot explore.

MAN is not, perhaps, so ignorant of anything, or any creature, as of himself. His own system, after all the art and inquisition of human ingenuity, is still to him the profoundest mystery in nature. His knowledge and faculties are adequate to the sphere of his duty. Beyond this, his researches are impertinent, and all his acquisitions useless. He has no adequate notions what the laws of the universe are with respect to any species of existence whatever. A cloud rests on the complicated movements of this great machine, which baffles all the penetration of mortals: and it will for ever remain impossible for man, from the most complete analysis of his present situation, to judge, with any degree of precision, of his own consequence, either as a citizen of the world at large, or as a member of any particular society. {47}

FINAL causes form a system of knowledge too wonderful for man. It is the perrogative of nature alone to decide upon them. In the fulness of time, her creative hand brought him into existence, and it belongs to her alone, in consequence of an arrangement equally wonderful and mysterious to dismiss him from his present mode of being. This is an authority with which she alone is invested, and which, according to our apprehensions, it is impossible fro her to delegate. Dissolution, as well as creation, is hers. and he who would attempt to infringe her sovereignty in this instance, would usurp a prerogative which does not belong to him, and become a traitor to the laws of his being. Nay, on this extravagant and licentious hypothesis, the right of assuming and relinquishing existence is made reciprocal. For he who arrogates the liberty of destroying himself, were he possessed of the power, might also be his own creator; his imaginary insignificance to society being as inconclusive in the one case, as any chimerical advantage that may accidentally strike him can be in the other. It is a strange doctrine, which cannot be established, but at the obvious expence of what seem the plainest dictates of common sense.

INDEED, the absurdities of this daring and paradoxical doctrine are endless and infinite. {48} When we come to pronounce on the condition of human infancy, and to separate childhood, or non–age, from a state of maturity, we can scarce trace one useful or salutary consequence it is calculated to produce in society. In this view children seem less adapted to serve any special or important end, than even beetles, gnats, or flies. Experience, however, has long convinced the world of their present inestimable value from their future destination. And were a legislator, from the plausible pretext of their being a burden to the state, to exterminate the race of mankind in the insignificant stage of infancy, his decree, like that of a certain monster recorded in the gospel, would shock the sentiments of every nation under heaven, in whom there remained only the dregs of humanity.

IT is not only impossible for a man to decide, in any given period, of the progress of his existence, or what utility or consequence he may be to society; but without the faculty of prescience, it is still more impracticable for him to divine what purposes he may be intended to serve in the many mysterious revolations of futurity. How far his mortal may be connected with his immortal life, must rest with him who has the sole disposal of it. But who told him that his load of misery was too much to bear, that he was not able to sustain {49} it? or that his merciful father would not proportionate his sufferings to his abilities? How does he know how short–lived the pressure of incumbent sorrow may prove? It becomes not him to prescribe to his maker, or because his evils are enormous, to conclude they must be permanent. Rash man! thy heart is in the hand of heaven, and he , may either lighten the burthen that oppresses thee, or blunt the edge of that sensibility, from which it derives the greatest poignancy. What medicine is to the wounds of the body, that resignation is to those of the soul. Be not deficient in this virtue, and life will never prescribe a duty you cannot perform, or inflict a pang which you cannot bear. Resignation changes the grizzly aspect of affliction, turns sickness into health, and converts the gloomy forebodings of despair into the grateful presentiments of hope. Besides, the most insignificant instruments are sometimes, in the hands of eternal providence, employed in bringing about the most general and beneficent revolutions. It is by making weakness thus subservient to power, evil to good, and pain to pleasure, that he who governs the world illustrates his sovereinty and omnipotence. Till, then, thou art {50} able to comprehend the whole mysterious system of every possible existence, till thou art certain that thy life is totally insignificant, till thou art convinced it is not in the might of infinite power to render thee serviceable either to thyself or others, counteract not the benignity of providence by suicide, or, in this manner, by the blackest of all treasons, betray thy trust, and wage, at fearful odds, hostility against the very means and author of thy being.

ONE very obvious consequence arising from suicide, which none of its advocates appear to have foreseen, and which places it in a light exceedingly gross and shocking, is, that it supposes every man capable, not only of destroying himself, but of delegating the power of committing murder to another. That which he may do himself, he may commission any one to do for him. On this supposition, no law, human or divine, could impeach the shedding of innocent blood. And on what principle, of right or expediency, admit that which produces such a train of the most horrid and detestable consequences?

(5) THE preceding note is, perhaps, the most audacious part in the whole of this very extraordinary performance. In our holy religion it is expressly declared that no murderer hath eternal life abiding in him; that murderers shall in no wise inherit the kingdom of God, and that it is the prerogative of heaven alone to kill and make alive. It is a fundamental {51} doctrine in the gospel, that, except ye repent, ye shall all likewise perish. And how are they to perform their duty, who, in the instant of dying, contract a guilt, which renders it indispensible. But this horrid supposition is repugnant to the whole genius of revelation, which inculcates every virtue that can possibly administer to our present and future welfare. It inforces obedience and resignation to the righteous government of God. It inspires and produces those very dispositions which it recommends. All its doctrines, exhortations, and duties, are formed to elevate the mind, to raise the affections, to regulate the passions, and to purge the heart of whatever is hostile to happiness in this or another life. This impious slander on the christian faith is the obvious consequence of the grossest inattention to its nature and tendency. It is calculated chiefly to make us happy. And what happy man was ever yet chargeable with suicide? In short, we may as well say, that, because the physician does not expressly prohibit certain diseases in his prescriptions, the very diseases are authenticated by the remedies devised, on purpose to counteract them. {52}

IMMORTALITY OF THE SOUL.

ESSAYS ON SUICIDE AND THE IMMORTALITY

(1) The ingenuity of Scepticism has been long admired, but here the author boldly outdoes all his former out–doings. Much has been said against the authenticity of religion, on the supposition that the evidence to which she appeals, is not either sufficiently general or intelligible to the bulk of mankind. But surely an argument is not conclusive in one case, and inconclusive in another. Admit this reasoning against revelation to be valid, and you must also admit it against our author's hypothesis. There never at least was an objection started, that could, in the remotest degree, affect the truths of the gospel, more intricate, metaphysical, and abstracted, than that by which our essayest would destroy the popular doctrine of the soul's . How many live and die in this salutary conviction, to whom these refined speculations must forever remain as unintelligible as if they had {53} never been formed! It is a sentiment so congenial to the heart of man, that few of the species would chuse to exist without it. Unable, as they are, to account for its origin, they cordially and universally indulge it, as one of their tenderest, best, and last feelings. It inhabits alike the rudest and most polished minds, and never leaves any human breast, which is not either wholly engrossed by criminal pleasure, deadened by selfish pursuits, or perverted by false reasoning. It governs with all the ardor and influence of inspiration, and never meets with any opposition but from the weak, the worthless, or the . All the world have uniformly considered it as their last resource in every extremity, and for the most part still regard and cherish the belief of it, as an asylum in which their best interests are ultimately secured or deposited, beyond the reach of all temporary disaster or misfortune. Where, therefore, is the probability of exterminating so popular and prevailing a notion, by a concatenation of ideas, which, perhaps, not one out of a million in any country under Heaven is able to trace or comprehend?

(2) The natural perceptions of pleasure of pain cannot be said to act on the mind as one part of matter does on another. The substance of the soul we do not know, but are {54} certain her ideas must be immaterial. And these cannot possibly act either by contact of impulse. When one body impels another, the body moved is affected only by the impulse. But the mind, whenever roused by any pleasing or painful sensation, in most cases looks round her, and deliberates whether a change of state is proper, or the present more eligible; and moves or rests accordingly. Her perceptions, therefore, contribute no further to action, than by exciting her active powers. On the contrary, matter is blindly and obstinately in that state in which it is, whether of motion or rest, till changed by some other adequate cause. Suppose we rest the state of any body, some external force is requisite to put it in motion; and, in proportion as this force is greater or small, the motion

must be swift or slow. Did not this body continue in its former state, no external force would be requisite to change it; nor, when changed, would different degrees of force be necessary to move it in different degrees of velocity. When motion is impressed on any body, to bring it to rest, an force must always be applied, in proportion to the intended effect. This resistance is observeable in bodies both when moved in particular directions, and to bear an exact proportion to the , and to the quantity of matter moved. Were it possible to extract from matter the qualities of solidity and extension, {55} the matter whence such qualities were extracted would no longer resist; and consequently resistance is the necessary result of them, which, therefore, in all directions must be the same. The degree of resistance in any body being proportionate to the , it follows, when that body is considered in any particular state, whether of motion or rest, the degrees of resistance must either indefinitely multiply, or decrease, according to all possible degrees of the moving force. But when the same body is considered absolutely, or without fixing any particular state, the resistance is immutable; and all the degrees of it, which that body would exert upon the accession of any impressed force, must be conceived as actually in it. Nor can matter have any tendency contrary to that resistance, otherwise it must be equal or superior. If equal, the two contrary tendencies would destroy each other. If superior, the resistance would be destroyed. Thus change would eternally succeed to change without one intermediate instant, so that no time would be assigned when any body was in any particular state. Gravitation itself, the most simple and universal law, seems far from being a tendency natural to matter; since it is found to act internally, and not in proportion to the superfices of any body; which it would not do, if it were only the mechanical action of matter upon matter. {56} From all this, it appears, that matter considered merely as such, is so far from having a principle of spontaneous motion, that it is stubbornly inactive, and must eternally remain in the same state in which it happens to be, except influenced by some other — that is, some immaterial power. Of such a power the human soul is evidently possessed; for every one is conscious of an internal activity, and to dispute this would be to dispute us out of one of the most real and intimate perceptions we have.

Though a material automaton were allowed possible, how infinitely would it fall short of that force and celerity which every one feels in himself. how sluggish are all the movements which fall under our observation. How slow and gradual their transitions from one part of space to another. But the mind, by one instantaneous effort, measures the distance from pole to pole, from heaven to earth, from one fixed star to another; and not confined within the limits of the visible creation, shoots into immensity with a rapidity to which even that of lightning, or sunbeams, is no comparison. Who then shall assign a period, which, though depressed with so much dead weight, is ever active, and unconscious of fatigue or relaxation? The mind is not only herself a principle of action, but probably actuates the body, without the {57} assistance of any intermediate power, both from the gradual command which she acquires of its members by habit, and from a capacity of determining, in some measure, the quantity of pleasure or pain which any sensible perception can give her. Supposing the interposing power a spirit, the same difficulty of spirit acting upon matter still remains. And the volition of our own mind will as well account for the motion of the body, as the formal interference of any other spiritual substance. And we may as well ask, why the mind is not conscious of that interposition, as why she is ignorant of the means by which she communicates motion to the body.

(3) It is always bad reasoning to draw conclusions from the premises not denied by your adversary. Whoever, yet, of all the assertors of the soul's immortality, presumed to make a monopoly of this great privilege to the human race? Who can tell what another state of existence may be, or whether every other species of animals may not possess principles an immortal as the mind of man? But that mode of reasoning, which militates against all our convictions, solely on account of the unavoidable ignorance to which our sphere in the universe subjects us, can never be satisfactory. Reason, it is true, cannot altogether solve every doubt which arises concerning this important truth. But neither is there any other {58} truth, of any denomination whatever, against which sophistry may not conjure up a multitude of exceptions. We know no mode of existence but those of matter and spirit, neither of which have uniformly and successfully defied the extreme subtilty of argumentation. Still a very great majority of mankind are staunch believers in both. So well constituted is the present disposition of things, that all the principles essential to human life and happiness continue, as it is likely they ever will, to operate, in spite of every sort of clamour which sophistry or scepticism has raised or can raise against them.

(4) There is not a single word in all this elaborate and tedious deduction, which has not been urged and refuted five hundred times. Our ignorance of the divine perfections, as is usual with this writer, is here stated as an unanswerable exception to the conclusion usually drawn from them. But he very artfully overlooks, that this great ignorance will be equally conclusive as applied to either side of the argument. When we compare, however, the character of God, as a wise superintendant, and generous benefactor, with the state in which things at present appear, where virtue is often depressed and afflicted, and vice

apparently triumphs, it will be treated with the infamy it merits, and virtue receive that {59} happiness and honour, which, from its own intrinsic worth, it deserves, and, from its conformity to the nature of God, it has reason to expect.

This subject, perhaps, has been too much exaggerated, and some pious men have weakly thought, the best way to convince us that order and happiness prevailed in a future state, was to persuade us that there was none at all in this. External advantages have been taken for the only goods of human nature; and, because, in this view, all things speak the appearance of mal–administration, we have been taught to expect a government of rectitude and benevolence hereafter. Let us, on the contrary, candidly own that virtue is sovereignly and solely good, left, by depreciating her charms, we obliquely detract from the character of God himself. Let us confess her undowered excellence superior to all the inconveniences that may attend her, even in the present situation. But, without allowing some difference between poverty and riches, sickness and health, pain and pleasure, we shall have no foundation to preference; and it will be in vain to talk of selecting where no one choice can be more agreeable or disagreeable to nature than another. Upon this difference, therefore, however it be called, let the present argument proceed. {60}

If infinite goodness be the spirit and characteristic of this universal government, then every advantage, however inconsiderable in kind or degree, must either be supposed immediately bestowed on virtue; or, at least, that such retributions will, at some time, be made her, as may not only render her votaries equal, but superior to those of vice, in proportion to their merit. But how different the case is in human life, history and observation may easily convince us; so that one, whose eyes are not intent on the character of God, and the nature of virtue, would often be tempted to think this world a theatre merely intended for mournful spectacles and pomps of horror. How many persons do we see perish by the mere wants of nature, who, had they been in different circumstances, would have thanked God with tears of joy for the power of communicating those advantages they now implore from others in vain? While, at the same time, they have, perhaps, the additional misery of seeing the most endeared relations involved in the same deplorable fate! How often do we see those ties which unite the soul and body, worn out by the gradual advances of a lingering disease, or burst at once by the sudden efforts of unutterable agony? While the unhappy sufferers, had they been continued in life, might have diffused happiness, not only through the narrow circle of their {61} friends and neighbourhood, but as extensively as their country, and even the world at large. How many names do we see buried in obscurity, or soiled with detraction, which ought to have shone the first in fame? How many heroes have survived the liberties of their country, or died in abortive attempts to preserve them; and, by their fall, only left a larger field for the lawless ravages of tyranny and oppression?

But were it possible, how long and insuperable would be the task to enumerate all the ingredients which compose the present cup of bitterness? And is this the consummation of things? Will supreme and essential goodness no way distinguish such as have invariably pursued his honour, and the interest of his government, from those who have industriously violated the order he has appointed in things? who have blotted the face of nature with havock, murder, and desolation; and shewn a constant intention to counteract all the benevolent designs of providence? It is confessed that the virtuous, happy in the possession of virtue alone, make their exit from the present scene with blessings to the Creator, for having called them to existence, and given them the glorious opportunity of enjoying what is in itself supremely eligible. They are conscious that this felicity can receive no accession from any external lustre or advantage {62} whatever. Yet it seems highly necessary in the divine administration, that those who have been dazzled with the false glare of prosperous wickedness, should at last be undeceived; that they should at last behold virtue conspicuous, in all her native splendor and majesty as she shines, the chief delight of God, and ultimate happiness of all intelligent nature.

The language of religion, and our own hearts, on this important argument, is equally comfortable and decisive. It accumulates and enforces whatever can inspire us with confidence in that God, who is not the God of the dead, but of the living; who reigns in the invisible, as well as in the visible world; and whose attention to our welfare ceases not with our lives, but is commensurate to the full extent of our being. Indeed the votaries of the soul's mortality may as well be honest for once, and speak out what so many fools think in their hearts. For what is God to us, or we to him, if our connection extends but to the pitiful space allotted us in such a pitiful world as this is? To be sure, no absurdity will be rejected, which can smother the feelings, or keep the vices of profligates in countenance; but, if only made like worms and reptiles beneath our feet, to live this moment, and expire the next, to struggle in a wretched life with every internal and external calamity, {63} that can assault our bodies, or infest our minds; to bear the mortifications of malignity, and the unmerited abhorrence of those who perhaps may owe us the greatest and tenderest esteem, and then, sunk in everlasting oblivion, our fate would stand on record, in the annals of the universe, an eternal exception to all that can be called good.

Suppose a father possessed of the most exquisite tenderness for his son, delighted with his similarity of form, his promising constitution, his strength, gracefulness, and agility, his undisguised emotions of filial affection, with the various presages of a superior genius and understanding. Let us suppose this father pleased with the employment of improving his faculties, and inspiring him with future hopes of happiness and dignity: but that he may give him a quicker sensibility to the misfortunes of others, and a more unshaken fortitude to sustain his own, he often prefers younger brethren, and even strangers, to those advantages which otherwise merit, and the force of nature would determine him to bestow on so worthy an offspring. Let us go further, and imagine, if we can, that this father, without the least diminution of tenderness, or any other apparent reason, destroys his son in the bloom of life, and height of expectation: Who would not lament the fate of such a youth with inconsolable tears? {64} Doomed never more to behold the agreeable light of Heaven! never more to display his personal graces, nor exercise his manly powers, never more to feel his heart warm with benevolent regards, nor taste the soul-transporting pleasure of obliging and being obliged! Blotted at once from existence, and the fair creation, he sinks into silence and oblivion, with all his sublime hopes disappointed, all his immense desires ungratified, and all his intellectual faculties unimproved. Without mentioning the instinctive horror which must attend such an action, how absurd to reason, and how inconsistent with the common feelings of humanity would it be to suppose a father capable of such a deed. Forbid it, God! forbid it, Nature! that we should impute to the munificent father of being and happiness, what, even in the lowest of rational creatures, would be monstrous and detestable!

(5) The truth is, that form which all mankind have deemed immortal, is so far from being the frailest, that it seems in fact the most indissoluble and permanent of any other we know. All the rational and inventive powers of the mind happily conspire to proclaim her infinitely different in nature, and superior in dignity to every possible modification of pure matter. Were mankind {65} joined in society, was life polished and cultivated, were the sciences and arts, not only of utility, but elegance, produced by matter? by a brute mass? A substance so contrary to all activity and intelligence, that it seems the work of an omnipotent hand alone to connect them. What judgement should we form of that principle which informed and enlightened a Galileo, a Copernicus, or a Newton? What inspiration taught them, to place the fun in the center of this system, and assign the various orbs their revolutions round him, reducing motions so diverse and unequal, to uniform and simple laws? Was it not something like that great eternal mind, which first gave existence to those luminous orbs, and prescribed each of them their province?

Whence the infinite harmony and variety of sound, the copious flows of eloquence, the bolder graces and more inspired elevations of poetry, but from a mind, an immaterial being, the reflected image of her all–perfect Creator, in whom eternally dwells all beauty and excellence. Were man only endowed with a principle of vegetation, fixed to one peculiar spot, and insensible of all that passed around him; we might, then, with some colour, suppose that energy, if it may be so called, perishable. Were, he like animals possessed of mere vitality, and qualified only to move and feel, still we might have some reason to fear that, {66} in some future period of duration, our Creator might resume his gift of existence. but can any one, who pretends to the least reflection, imagine that such a being as the human soul, adorned with such extensive intellectual powers, will ever cease to be the object of that love and care which eternally holds the universe in its embrace? Did she obtain such a boundless understanding merely to taste the pleasure of exercising it? to catch a transient glance of its objects, and perish? Formed, as she is, to operate on herself, and all things round her, must she cease from action, while yet the mighty task is scarce begun? must she lose those faculties, by which she retains the past, comprehends the presents and presages the future? must she contemplate no more those bright impressions of divinity, which are discovered in the material world; nor those stronger, and more animated features of the same eternal beauty which shine in her own god–like form? And must she be absorbed forever in the womb of unessential nothing? Strange, that in the view, and even in the arms of infinite power and goodness, a dawn so fair and promising, should at one be clouded with all the horrors of eternal night? Such a supposition would be contrary the whole conduct and laws of nature. {67}

SUICIDE ROSSEAU's ELOISA.

LETTER CXIV.

YES, my Lord, I confess it; the weight of life is too heavy for my soul. I have long endured it as a burden; I have lost every thing which could make it dear to me, and nothing remains but irksomeness and vexation. I am told, however, that I am not at liberty to dispose of my life, without the permission of that Being from whom I received it. I am sensible likewise that you have a right over it by more titles than one. Your care has twice preserved it, and your goodness is its constant security. I will never {68} dispose of it, till I am certain that I may do it without a crime, and till I have not the least hope of employing it for your service.

ESSAYS ON SUICIDE AND THE IMMORTALITY

You told me that I should be of use to you; why did you deceive me? Since we have been in London, so far from thinking of employing me in your concerns, you have been kind enough to make me your only concern. How superfluous is your obliging solicitude! My lord, you know I abhor a crime, even worse than I detest life; I adore the supreme Being — I owe every thing to you; I have an affection for you; you are the only person on earth to whom I am attached. Friendship and duty may chain a wretch to this earth: sophistry and vain pretences will never detain him. Enlighten my understanding, speak to my heart; I am ready to hear you, but remember, that despair is not to be imposed upon.

You would have me apply to the test of reason: I will; let us reason. You desire me to deliberate in proportion to the importance {69} of the question in debate; I agree to it. Let us investigate truth with temper and moderation; let us discuss this general proposition with the same indifference we should treat any other. Roebeck wrote an apology for suicide before he put an end to his life. I will not, after his example, write a book on the subject, neither am I well satisfied with that which he has penned, but I hope in this discussion at least to imitate his moderation.

I have for a long time meditated on this awful subject. You must be sensible that I have, for you know my destiny, and yet I am alive. The more I reflect, the more I am convinced that the question may be reduced to this fundamental proposition. Every man has a right by nature to pursue what he thinks good, and avoid what he thinks evil, in all respects which are not injurious to others. When our life therefore becomes a misery to ourselves, and is of advantage to no one, we are at liberty to put an end to our being. If there is any such thing as a clear and self−evident {70} principle, certainly this is one, and if this be subverted, there is scarce an action in life which may not be made criminal.

Let us hear what the philosophers say on this subject. First, they consider life as something which is not our own, because we hold it as a gift; but because it has been given to us, is it for that reason our own? Has not God given these sophists two arms? nevertheless, when they are under apprehensions of a mortification, they do not scruple to amputate one, or both if there be occasion. By a parity of reasoning, we may convince those who believe in the immortality of the soul; for if I sacrifice my arm to the preservation of something more precious, which is my body, I have the same right to sacrifice my body to the preservation of something more valuable, which is, the happiness of my existence. If all the gifts which heaven has bestowed are naturally designed for our good, they are certainly too apt to change their nature; and Providence has endowed us with reason, that we may discern the difference. If this rule {71} did not authorize us to chuse the one, and reject the other, to what use would it serve among mankind?

But they turn this weak objection into a thousand shapes. They consider a man living upon earth as a soldier placed on duty. God, say they, has fixed you in this world, why do you quit your station without his leave? But you, who argue thus, has he not stationed you in the town where you was born, why therefore do you quit it without his leave? is not misery, of itself, a sufficient permission? Whatever station Providence has assigned me, whether it be in a regiment, or on the earth at large, he intended me to stay there while I found my situation agreeable, and to leave it when it became intolerable. This is the voice of nature, and the voice of God. I agree that we must wait for an order; but when I die a natural death, God does not order me to quit life, he takes it from me; it is by rendering life insupportable, that he orders me to quit it. In the first case, I resist with all my force; in the second, I have the merit of obedience. {72}

Can you conceive that there are some people so absurd as to arraign suicide as a kind of rebellion against Providence, by an attempt to fly from his laws? but we do not put an end to our being in order to withdraw ourselves from his commands, but to execute them. What! does the power of God extend no farther than to my body? is there a spot in the universe, is there any being in the universe, which is not subject to his power, and will that power have less immediate influence over me when my being is refined, and thereby becomes less compound, and of nearer resemblance to the divine essence? no, his justice and goodness are the foundation of my hopes; and if I thought that death would withdraw me from his power, I would give up my resolution to die.

This is one of the quibbles of the Phaedo, which, in other respects, abounds with sublime truths. If your slave destroys himself, says Socrates to Cebes, would you not punish him, for having unjustly deprived you of your property; {73} prithee, good Socrates, do we not belong to God after we are dead? The case you put is not applicable; you ought to argue thus: if you incumber your slave with a habit which confines him from discharging his duty properly, will you punish him for quitting it, in order to render you better service? the grand error lies in making life of too great importance; as if our existence depended upon it, and that death was a total annihilation. Our life is of no consequence in the sight of God; it is of no importance in the eyes of reason, neither ought it to be of any in our sight; when we quit our body, we only lay aside an inconvenient habit. Is this circumstance so painful, to be the occasion of so much disturbance? My Lord, these declaimers are not in earnest. Their arguments are absurd and cruel, for they aggravate the supposed crime, as if it put a period to existence, and they punish it, as if that existence was eternal.

With respect to Plato's Phaedo, which has furnished them with the only specious argument that has ever been advanced, the question {74} is discussed there in a very light and desultory manner. Socrates being condemned, by an unjust judgment, to lose his life in a few hours, had no occasion to enter into an accurate enquiry whether he was at liberty to dispose of it himself. Supposing him really to have been the author of those discourses which Plato ascribes to him, yet believe me, my lord, he would have meditated with more attention on the subject, had he been in circumstances which required him to reduce his speculations to practice; and a strong proof that no valid objection can be drawn from that immortal work against the right of disposing of our own lives, is, that Cato read it twice through the very night that he destroyed himself.

The same sophisters make it a question whether life can ever be an evil? but when we consider the multitude of errors, torments, and vices, with which it abounds, one would rather be inclined to doubt whether it can ever be a blessing. Guilt incessantly besieges the most virtuous of mankind. Every moment he lives he is in danger of falling a prey to the wicked, or of being wicked himself. To {75} struggle and to endure, is his lot in this world; that of the dishonest man is to do evil, and to suffer. In every other particular they differ, and only agree in sharing the miseries of life in common. If you required authorities and facts, I could recite you the oracles of old, the answers of the sages, and produce instances where acts of virtue have been recompensed with death. But let us leave these considerations, my lord; it is to you whom I address myself, and I ask you what is the chief attention of a wise man in this life, except, if I may be allowed the expression, to collect himself inwardly, and endeavour, even while he lives, to be dead to every object of sense? The only way by which wisdom directs us to avoid the miseries of human nature, is it not to detach ourselves from all earthly objects, from every thing that is gross in our composition, to retire within ourselves, and to raise our thoughts to sublime contemplations? If therefore our misfortunes are derived from our passions and errors, with what eagerness should we wish for a state which will deliver us both from the one and the other? What is {76} the fate of those sons of sensuality, who indiscreetly multiply their torments by their pleasures? they in fact destroy their existence by extending their connections in this life; they increase the weight of their crimes by their numerous attachments; they relish no enjoyments, but what are succeeded by a thousand bitter wants; the more lively their sensibility, the more acute their sufferings; the stronger they are attached to life, the more wretched they become.

But admitting it, in general, a benefit to mankind to crawl upon the earth with gloomy sadness, I do not mean to intimate that the human race ought with one common consent to destroy themselves, and make the world one immense grave. But there are miserable beings, who are too much exalted to be governed by vulgar opinion; to them despair and grievous torments are the passports of nature. It would be as ridiculous to suppose that life can be a blessing to such men, as it was absurd in the sophister Possidonius to deny that is was an {77} evil, at the same time that he endured all the torments of the gout. While life is agreeable to us, we earnestly wish to prolong it, and nothing but a sense of extreme misery can extinguish the desire of existence; for we naturally conceive a violent dread of death, and this dread conceals the miseries of human nature from our sight. We drag a painful and melancholy life, for a long time before we can resolve to quit it; but when once life becomes so insupportable as to overcome the horror of death, then existence is evidently a great evil, and we cannot disengage ourselves from it too soon. Therefore, though we cannot exactly ascertain the point at which it ceases to be a blessing, yet at least we are certain in that it is an evil long before it appears to be such, and with every sensible man the right of quitting life is, by a great deal, precedent to the temptation.

This is not all. After they have denied that life can be an evil, in order to bar our right of making away with ourselves; they confess immediately afterwards that it is an {78} evil, by reproaching us with want of courage to support it. According to them, it is cowardice to withdraw ourselves from pain and trouble, and there are none but dastards who destroy themselves. O Rome, thou victrix of the world, what a race of cowards did thy empire produce! Let Arria, Eponina, Lucretia, be of the number; they were women. But Brutus, Cassius, and thou great and divine Cato, who didst share with the gods the adoration of an astonished world, thou whose sacred and august presence animated the Romans with holy zeal, and made tyrants tremble, little did thy proud admirers imagine that paltry rhetoricians, immured in the dusty corner of a college, would ever attempt to prove that thou wert a coward, for having preferred death to a shameful existence.

O the dignity and energy of your modern writers! How sublime, how intrepid are you with your pens? but tell me, thou great and valiant hero, who dost so courageously decline the battle, in order to endure the pain of living somewhat longer; when spark of fire {79} lights upon your hand, why do you withdraw it in such haste? how? are you such a coward that you dare not bear the scorching of fire? nothing, you say, can oblige you to endure the burning spark; and what obliges me to endure life? was the creation of a man of more difficulty to Providence, than that of a straw? and is not both one and the other equally the work of his hands?

Without doubt, it is an evidence of great fortitude to bear with firmness the misery which we cannot shun; none but a fool, however, will voluntarily endure evils which he can avoid without a crime; and it is very often a great crime to suffer pain unnecessarily. He who has not resolution to deliver himself from a miserable being by a speedy death, is like one who would rather suffer a wound to mortify, than trust to a surgeon's knife for his cure. Come, thou worthy — cut off this leg, which endangers my life. I will see it done without shrinking, and will give that hero leave to call me coward, who suffers his leg to mortify, because he dares not undergo the same operation. {80}

I acknowledge that there are duties owing to others, the nature of which will not allow every man to dispose of his life; but, in return, how many are there which give him a right to dispose of it? let a magistrate on whom the welfare of a nation depends, let a father of a family who is bound to procure subsistence for his children, let a debtor who might ruin his creditors, let these at all events discharge their duty; admitting a thousand other civil and domestic relations to oblige an honest and unfortunate man to support the misery of life, to avoid the greater evil of doing injustice; is it, therefore, under circumstances totally different, incumbent on us to preserve a life oppressed with a swarm of miseries, when it can be of no service but to him who has not courage to die? "Kill me, my child," says the decrepid savage to his son, who carries him on his shoulders, and bends under his weight; the "enemy is at hand; go to battle with thy brethren; go and preserve thy children, and do not suffer thy helpless father to fall {81} alive into the hands of those whose relations he has mangled." Though hunger, sickness, and poverty, those domestic plagues, more dreadful than savage enemies, may allow a wretched cripple to consume, in a sick bed, the provisions of a family which can scarce subsist itself, yet he who has no connections, whom heaven has reduced to the necessity of living alone, whose wretched existence can produce no good, why should not he, at least, have the right of quitting a station, where his complaints are troublesome, and his sufferings of no benefit?

Weigh these considerations, my lord; collect these arguments, and you will find that they may be reduced to the most simple of nature's rights, of which no man of sense ever yet entertained a doubt. In fact, why should we be allowed to cure ourselves of the gout, and not to get rid of the misery of life? do not both evils proceed from the same hand? to what purpose is it to say, that death is painful? are drugs agreeable to be taken? no, nature revolts against both. Let them prove therefore {82} that it is more justifiable to cure a transient disorder by the application of remedies, than to free ourselves from an incurable evil by putting an end to our life; and let them shew how it can be less criminal to use the bark for a fever, than to take opium for the stone. If we consider the object in view, it is in both cases to free ourselves from painful sensations; if we regard the means, both one and the other are equally natural; if we consider the repugnance of our nature, it operates equally on both sides; if we attend to the will of providence, can we struggle against any evil of which it is not the author can we deliver ourselves from any torment which the hand of God has not inflicted? what are the bounds which limit his power, and when resistance lawful? are we then to make no alteration in the condition of things, because every thing is in the state he appointed? must we do nothing in this life, for fear of infringing his laws, or is it in our power to break them if we would? no, my lord, the occupation of man is more great and noble. God did not give him life that he should supinely {83} remain in a state of constant inactivity. But he gave him freedom to act, conscience to will, and reason to choose what is good. He has constituted him sole judge of all his actions. He has engraved this precept in his heart, Do whatever you conceive to be for your own good, provided you thereby do no injury to others. If my sensations tell me that death is eligible, I resist his orders by an obstinate resolution to live; for, by making death desirable, he directs me to put an end to my being.

My lord, I appeal to your wisdom and candour; what more infallible maxims can reason deduce from religion, with respect to suicide? If Christians have adopted contrary tenets, they are neither drawn from the principles of religion, nor from the only sure guide, the Scriptures, but borrowed from the Pagan philosophers. Lactantius and Augustine, the first who propagated this new doctrine, of which Jesus Christ and his apostles take no notice, ground their arguments entirely on the reasoning of Phaedo, which I have already {84} controverted; so that the believers, who, in this respect, think they are supported by the authority of the Gospel, are in fact only countenanced by the authority of Plato. In truth, where do we find, throughout the whole bible any law against suicide, or so much as a bare disapprobation of it; and is it not very unaccountable, that among the instances produced of persons who devoted themselves to death, we do not find the least word of improbation against examples of this kind? nay, what is more, the instance of Samson's voluntary death is authorized by a miracle, by which he revenges himself of his enemies. Would this miracle have been displayed to justify a crime; and would this man, who lost his strength by suffering himself to be seduced by the allurements of a woman, have recovered it to commit an authorised crime, as if God himself would practice deceit on men?

Thou shalt do no murder, says the decalogue; what are we to infer from this? if this commandment is to be taken literally, we {85} must not destroy malefactors, nor our enemies: and Moses, who put so many people to death, was a bad interpreter of his own precept. If there are any exceptions, certainly the first must be in favour of suicide, because it is exempt from any degree of violence and injustice, the two only circumstances which can make homicide criminal; and because nature, moreover, has, in this respect, thrown sufficient obstacles in the way.

But still they tell us, we must patiently endure the evils which God inflicts, and make a merit of our sufferings. This application however of the maxims of Christianity, is very ill calculated to satisfy our judgment. Man is subject to a thousand troubles, his life is a complication of evils, and he seems to have been born only to suffer. Reason directs him to shun as many of these evils as he can avoid; and religion, which is never in contradiction to reason, approves of his endeavours. But how inconsiderable is the account of these evils, in comparison with those he is obliged to endure against his will? It is with {86} respect to these, that a merciful God allows man to claim the merit of resistance; he receives the tribute he has been pleased to impose, as a voluntary homage, and he places our resignation in this life to our profit in the next. True repentance is derived from nature; if man endures whatever he is obliged to suffer, he does, in this respect, all that God requires of him; and if any one is so inflated with pride, as to attempt more, he is a madman, who ought to be confined, or an impostor, who ought to be punished. Let us, therefore, without scruple, fly from all the evils we can avoid; there will still be too many left for us to endure. Let us, without remorse, quit life itself when it becomes a torment to us, since it is in our own power to do it, and that in so doing we neither offend God nor man. If we would offer a sacrifice to the supreme Being, is it nothing to undergo death? let us devote to God that which he demands by the voice of reason, and into his hands let us peaceably surrender our souls.

Such are the liberal precepts which good {87} sense dictates to every man, and which religion authorises.[8] Let us apply these precepts to ourselves. You have condescended to disclose your mind to me; I am acquainted with your uneasiness; you do not endure less than myself; and your troubles, like mine, are incurable; and they are the more remediless, {88} as the laws of honour are more immutable than those of fortune. You bear them, I must confess, with fortitude. Virtue supports you; advance but one step farther, and she disengages you. You intreat me to suffer; my lord, I dare importune you to put an end to your sufferings; and I leave you to judge which of us is most dear to the other.

Why should we delay doing that which we must do at last? shall we wait till old age and decrepid baseness attach us to life, after they have robbed it of its charms, and till we are doomed to drag an infirm and decrepid body with labour, and ignominy, and pain? We are at an age when the soul has vigour to disengage itself with ease from its shackles, and when a man knows how to die as he ought; when farther advanced in years, he suffers himself to be torn from life, which he quits with reluctance. Let us take advantage of this time, when the tedium of life makes death desirable; and let us tremble for fear it should come in all its horrors, at the moment when we could wish to avoid it. I remember {89} the time, when I prayed to heaven only for a single hour of life, and when I should have died in despair if it had not been granted. Ah! what a pain it is to burst asunder the ties which attach our hearts to this world, and how advisable it is to quit life the moment the connection is broken! I am sensible, my lord, that we are both worthy of a purer mansion; virtue points it out, and destiny invites us to seek it. May the friendship which invites us preserve our union to the latest hour! O what a pleasure for two sincere friends voluntary to end their days in each others arms, to intermingle their latest breath, and at the same instant to give up the soul which they shared in common! What pain, what regret can infect their last moments? What do they quit by taking leave of the world? They go together; they quit nothing. {90}

LETTER CXV.

ANSWER.

THOU art distracted, my friend, by a fatal passion; be more discreet; do not give counsel, whilst thou standest so much in need of advice. I have known greater evils than yours. I am armed with fortitude of mind; I am an Englishman, and not afraid to die; but I know how to live and suffer as becomes a man. I have seen death near at hand, and have viewed it with too much indifference to go in search of it.

It is true, I thought you might be of use to me; my affection stood in need of yours: your endeavours might have been serviceable to me; your understanding might have enlightened me in the most important concern of my life; if I do not avail myself of it, who are you to impute it to? Where is it? What {91} is become of it? What are you capable of? Of what use can you be in your present condition? What service can I expect from you? A senseless grief renders you stupid and unconcerned. Thou art no man; thou art nothing; and if I did not consider what thou mightest be, I cannot conceive any thing more abject.

There is need of no other proof than your letter itself. Formerly I could discover in you good sense and truth. Your sentiments were just, your reflections proper, and I liked you not only from judgment but choice; for I considered your influence as an additional motive to excite me to the study of wisdom. But what do I perceive now in the arguments of your letter, with which you appear to be so highly satisfied? A wretched and perpetual sophistry, which in the erroneous deviations of your reason shews the disorder of your mind, and which I would not stoop to refute, if I did not commiserate your delirium. {92}

To subvert all your reasoning with one word, I would only ask you a single question. You who believe in the existence of a God, in the immortality of the soul, and in the freewill of man, you surely cannot suppose that an intelligent being is embodied, and stationed on the earth by accident only, to exist, to suffer, and to die. It is certainly most probable that the life of man is not without some design, some end, some moral object. I intreat you to give me a direct answer to this point; after which we will deliberately examine your letter, and you will blush to have written it.

But let us wave all general maxims, about which we often hold violent disputes, without adopting any of them in practice; for in their applications we always find some particular circumstances which makes such an alteration in the state of things, that every one thinks himself dispensed from submitting to the rules which he prescribes to others; and it is well known, that every man who establishes {93} general principles deems them obligatory on all the world, himself excepted. Once more let us speak to you in particular.

You believe that you have a right to put an end to your being. Your proof is of a very singular nature; "because I am disposed to die, say you, I have a right to destroy myself." This is certainly a very convenient argument for villains of all kinds: they ought to be very thankful to you for the arms with which you have furnished them; there can be no crimes, which, according to your arguments, may not be justified by the temptation to perpetrate them; and as soon as the impetuosity of passion shall prevail over the horror of guilt, their disposition to do evil will be considered as a right to commit it.

Is it lawful for you therefore to quit life? I should be glad to know whether you have yet begun to live? what! was you placed here on earth to do nothing in this world? did not heaven when it gave you existence give you some task or employment? If you have {94} accomplished your day's work before evening, rest yourself for the remainder of the day; you have a right to do it; but let us see your work. What answer are you prepared to make the supreme Judge, when he demands an account of your time? Tell me, what can you say to him? — I have seduced a virtuous girl: I have forsaken a friend in distress. Thou unhappy wretch! point out to me that just man who can boast that he has lived long enough; let me learn from him in what manner I ought to have spent my days to be at liberty to quit life.

You enumerate the evils of human nature. You are not ashamed to exhaust common-place topics, which have been hackneyed over a hundred times; and you conclude that life is an evil. But search, examine into the order of things, and see whether you can find any good which is not intermingled with evil. Does it therefore follow that there is no good in the universe, and can you confound what is in its own nature evil, with that which is only an evil accidentally? You have {95} confessed yourself, that the transitory and passive life of man is of no consequence, and only bears respect to matter from which he will soon be disencumbered; but his active and moral life, which ought to have most influence over his nature, consists in the exercise of free-will. Life is an evil to a wicked man in prosperity, and a blessing to an honest man in distress: for it is not its casual modification, but its relation to some final object which makes it either good or bad. After all, what are these cruel torments which force you to abandon life? do you imagine, that under your affected impartiality in the enumeration of the evils of this life, I did not discover that you was ashamed to speak of your own? Trust me, and do not at once abandon every virtue. Preserve at least your wonted sincerity, and speak thus openly to your friend; "I have lost all hope of seducing a modest woman, I am oliged therefore to be a man of virtue; I had much rather die."

You are weary of living; and you tell me, that life is an evil. Sooner or later you will {96} receive consolation, and then you will say life is a blessing. You will speak with more truth, though not with better reason; for nothing will have altered but yourself. Begin the alteration then from this day; and, since all the evil you lament is in the disposition of your mind, correct your irregular appetites, and do not set your house on fire to avoid the trouble of putting it in order.

I endure misery, say you: Is it in my power to avoid suffering? But this is changing the state of the question: for the subject of enquiry is, not whether you suffer, but whether your life is an evil? Let us proceed. You are wretched, you naturally endeavour to extricate yourself from misery. Let us see whether, for that purpose, it is necessary to die.

Let us for a moment examine the natural tendency of the afflictions of the mind, as in direct opposition to the evils of the body, the two substances being of contrary nature. The latter become worse and more inveterate the {97} longer they continue, and at length utterly destroy this mortal machine. The former, on the contrary, being only external and transitory modifications of an immortal and uncompounded essence, are insensibly effaced, and leave the mind in its original form, which is not susceptible of alteration. Grief, disquietude, regret, and despair, are evils of short duration, which never take root in the mind; and experience always falsifies that bitter reflection, which makes us imagine our misery will have no end. I will go farther; I cannot imagine that the vices which contaminate us, are more inherent in our nature than the troubles we endure; I not only believe that they perish with the body which gives them birth, but I think, beyond all doubt, that a longer life would be sufficient to reform mankind, and that many ages of youth would teach us that nothing is preferable to virtue.

However this may be, as the greatest part of our physical evils are incessantly encreasing, the acute pains of the body, when they are incurable, may justify a man's destroying himself; {98} for all his faculties being distracted with pain, and the evil being without remedy, he has no longer any use either of his will or of his reason; he ceases to be a man before he is dead, and does nothing more in taking away his life, than quit a body which incumbers him, and in which his soul is no longer resident.

But it is otherwise with the afflictions of the mind, which, let them be ever so acute, always carry their remedy with them. In fact, what is it that makes any evil intolerable? Nothing but its duration. The operations of surgery are generally much more painful than the disorders they cure; but the pain occasioned by the latter is lasting, that of the operation is momentary, and therefore preferable. What occasion is there therefore for any operation to remove troubles which die of course by their duration, the only circumstance which could render them insupportable? Is it reasonable to apply such desperate remedies to evils which expire of themselves? To a man who values himself on his fortitude, {99} and who estimates years at their real value, of two ways by which he may extricate himself from the same troubles, which will appear preferable, death or time? Have patience, and you will be cured. What would you desire more?

Oh! you will say, it doubles my afflictions to reflect that they will cease at last! This is the vain sophistry of grief! an apophthegm void of reason, of propriety, and perhaps of sincerity. What an absurd motive of despair is the hope of terminating misery![9] Even allowing this fantastical reflection, who would not chuse to encrease the present pain for a moment, under the assurance of putting an end to it, as we scarify a wound in order to heal it? and admitting any charm in grief, to make us in love with suffering, {100} when we release ourselves from it by putting an end to our being, do we not at that instant incur all that we apprehend hereafter?

Reflect thoroughly, young man; what are ten, twenty, thirty years, in competition with immortality? Pain and pleasure pass like a shadow; life slides away in an instant; it is nothing of itself; its value depends on the use we make of it. The good that we have done is all that remains, and it is that alone which marks its importance.

Therefore do not say any more that your existence is an evil, since it depends upon yourself to make it a blessing; and if it be an evil to have lived, this is an additional reason for prolonging life. Do not pretend neither to say any more that you are at liberty to die; for it is as much as to say that you have power to alter your nature, that you have a right to revolt against the author of your being, and to frustrate the end of your existence. But when you add, that your death does injury to {101} no one, do you recollect that you make this declaration to your friend?

Your death does injury to no one? I understand you! You think the loss I shall sustain by your death of no importance; you deem my affliction of no consequence. I will urge to you no more the rights of friendship, which you despise; but are there not obligations still more dear,[10] which ought to induce you to preserve your life? If there be a person in the world who loved you to that degree as to be unwilling to survive you, and whose happiness depends on yours, do you think that you have no obligations to her? Will not the execution of your wicked design disturb the peace of a mind, which has been with such difficulty restored to its former innocence? Are not you afraid to add fresh torments to a heart of such sensibility? Are not you apprehensive left your death should be attended {102} with a loss more fatal, which would deprive the world and virtue itself of its brightest ornament? And if she should survive you, are not you afraid to rouse up remorse in her bosom, which is more grievous to support than life itself? Thou ungrateful friend! thou indelicate lover! wilt thou always be taken up wholly with thyself? Wilt thou always think on thy own troubles alone? Hast thou no regard for the happiness of one who was so dear to thee? and cannot thou resolve to live for her who was willing to die with thee?

You talk of the duties of a magistrate, and of a father of a family: and because you are not under those circumstances, you think yourself absolutely free. And are you then under no obligations to society, to whom you are indebted for your preservation, your talents, your understanding? do you owe nothing to your native country, and to those unhappy people who may need your existence! O what an accurate calculation you make! among the obligations you have enumerated, {103} you have only omitted those of a man and of a citizen. Where is the virtuous patriot, who refused to enlist under a foreign prince, because his blood ought not to be split but in the service of his country; and who now, in a fit of despair, is ready to shed it against the express prohibition of the laws? The laws, the laws, young man! did any wife man ever despise them? Socrates, though innocent, out of regard to them refused to quit his prison. You do not scruple to violate them by quitting life unjustly; and you ask, what injury do I?

You endeavour to justify yourself by example. You presume to mention the Romans: you talk of the Romans! it becomes you indeed to cite those illustrious names. Tell me, did Brutus die a lover in despair, and did Cato plunge the dagger in his breast for his mistress? Thou weak and abject man! what resemblance is there between Cato and thee? Shew me the common standard between that sublime soul and thine. Ah vain wretch! hold thy peace: I am afraid to profane {104} his name by a vindication of his conduct. At that august and sacred name every friend to virtue should bow to the ground, and honour the memory of the greatest hero in silence.

How ill you have selected your examples, and how meanly you judge of the Romans, if you imagine that they thought themselves at liberty to quit life so soon as it became a burden to them. Recur to the excellent days of that republic, and seen whether you will find a single citizen of virtue, who thus freed himself from the discharge of his duty even after the most cruel misfortunes. When Regulus was on his return to Carthage, did he prevent the torments which he knew were preparing for him by destroying himself? What would not Posthumus have given, when obliged to pass under the yoke at Caudium, had this resource been justifiable? How much did even the senate admire that effort of courage, which enabled the consul Varro to survive his defeat? For what reason did so many generals voluntary surrender themselves to their enemies, they to whom ignominy was so dreadful, {105} and who were so little afraid of dying? It was because they considered their blood, their life, and their latest breath, as devoted to their country; and neither shame nor misfortune could dissuade them from this sacred duty. But when the laws were subverted, and the state became a prey to tyranny, the citizens resumed their natural liberty, and the right they had over their own lives. When Rome was no more, it was lawful for the Romans to give up their lives; they had discharged their duties on earth, they had no longer any country to defend, they were therefore at liberty to dispose of their lives, and to obtain that freedom for themselves which they could not recover for their country. After having spent their days in the service of expiring Rome, and in fighting for the defence of its laws, they died great virtuous as they had lived, and their death was an additional tribute to the glory of the Roman name, since none of them beheld a fight above all others most dishonourable, that of a true citizen stooping to an usurper. {106}

But thou, what art thou? what hast thou done? dost thou think to excuse thyself on account of thy obscurity? does thy weakness exempt thee from thy duty, and because thou hast neither rank nor distinction in thy country, art thou less subject to the laws? It becomes you vastly to presume to talk of dying while you owe the service of your life to your equals. Know, that a death, such as you meditate, is shameful and surreptitious. It is a theft committed on mankind in general. Before you quit life, return the benefits you have received from every individual. But, say you, I have no attachments; I am useless in the world. O thou young philosopher! art thou ignorant that thou canst not more a single step without finding some duty to fulfil; and that every man is useful to society, even by means of his existence alone?

Hear me, thou rash young man! thou art dear to me. I commiserate thy errors. If the least sense of virtue still remains in thy breast, attend, and let me teach thee to be reconciled {107} to life. Whenever thou art tempted to quit, say to thyself — "Let me do at least one good action before I die." Then go in search for one in a state of indigence, whom thou mayest relieve; for one under misfortunes, whom thou mayest comfort; for one under oppression, whom thou mayest defend. Introduce to me those unhappy wretches whom my rank keeps at a distance. Do not be afraid of misusing my purse, or my credit: make free with them; distribute my fortune; make me rich. If this consideration restrains you to-day, it will restrain you to- morrow; if no to morrow, it will restrain you all your life. If it has no power to restrain you, die! you are below my care.

FINIS.

* * * *

[NOTES]

---

[1]De Divin. lib. ii.

[2]Agamus Die Gratias, quad nemo in vita teneri potest. SEN. Epist. 12.

[3]TACIT. Ann. lib i.

[4]IT would be easy to prove that suicide is as lawful under the Christian dispensation as it was to the Heathens. There is not a single text of scripture which prohibits it. That great and infallible rule of faith and practice which must controul all philosophy and human reasoning, has left us in this particular to our natural liberty. Resignation to Providence is indeed recommended in scripture; but that implies only submission to ills that are unavoidable, not to such as may be remedied by prudence or courage. , is evidently meant to exclude only the killing of others, over whose life we have no authority. That this precept, like most of the scripture precepts, must be modified by reason and common sense, is plain from the practice of magistrates, who punish criminals capitally, notwithstanding the letter of the law. But were this commandment ever so express against suicide, it would now have no authority, for all the law of is abolished, except so far as it is established by the law of nature. And we have already endeavoured to prove that suicide is not prohibited by that law. In all cases Christians and Heathens are precisely upon the same footing; and , and acted heroically; those who now imitate their example

ought to receive the same praises from posterity. The power of committing suicide is regarded by as an advantage which men possess even above the Deity himself. "Deus non sibi potest mortem consciscere si velit quod homini dedit optimum in tantis vitae paenis." Lib. II. Cap. 7.

[5]Quint. Curtius lib. VI. cap. 5.

[6]Suet. Augus. cap. 3.

[7]Lib. 7. cap. 55.

[8]A strange letter this for the discussion of such a subject! Do men argue so cooly on a question of this nature, when they examine it on their own accounts? Is the letter a forgery, or does the author reason only with an intent to be refuted? What makes our opinion in this particular dubious, is the example of Robeck, which he cites, and which seems to warrant his own. Robeck deliberated so gravely that he had patience to write a book, a large, voluminous, weighty, and dispassionate book; and when he had concluded, according to his principles, that it was lawful to put an end to our being, he destroyed himself with the same composure that he wrote. Let us beware of the prejudices of the times, and of particular countries. When suicide is out of fashion we conclude that none but madmen destroy themselves; and all the efforts of courage appear chimerical to dastardly minds; every one judges of others by himself. Nevertheless, how many instances are there, well attested, of men, in every other respect perfectly discreet, who, without remorse, rage, or despair, have quitted life for no other reason than because it was a burden to them, and have died with more composure than they lived?

[9]No, my lord, we do not put an end to misery by these means, but rather fill the measure of affliction, by bursting asunder the last ties which attach us to felicity. When we regret what was dear to us, grief itself still attaches us to the object we lament, which is a state less deplorable than to be attached to nothing.

[10]Obligations more dear than those of friendship! Is it a philosopher who talks thus? But this affected sophist was of an amorous disposition.

Printed in the United States
74198LV00007B